How to start a staffing Placement business

A Strategic Agency Guide to Entrepreneurial Freedom: Launch, Grow and Manage Like a PRO; Dominate the Recruitment Industry with Proven Growth Hacks

Dan Blake

How to start a staffing placement business

How to start a staffing placement business

Copyright © 2024 by Dan Blake

All rights reserved. This book or parts thereof may not be reproduced in any form, stored in any retrieval system, or transmitted in any form by any means—electronic, mechanical, photocopy, recording, or otherwise—without prior written permission of the publisher.

How to start a staffing placement business

TABLE OF CONTENTS

Chapter 1: Introduction to Staffing Placement Business

Understanding the Staffing Industry

Benefits and Challenges of Starting a Staffing Agency

Overview of the Recruitment Process

Chapter 2: Market Research and Analysis

Identifying Target Markets and Niches

Analyzing Competitors and Industry Trends

Assessing Demand and Supply Dynamics

Chapter 3: Crafting Your Business Plan

Defining Your Business Model

Setting Goals and Objectives

Financial Planning and Projections

Chapter 4: Legal and Regulatory Compliance

Choosing the Right Legal Structure

Licensing and Permits

Compliance with Employment Laws and Regulations

Chapter 5: Building Your Brand

Developing a Unique Value Proposition

Creating a Compelling Brand Identity

Establishing an Online Presence

Chapter 6: Recruitment and Talent Acquisition

Sourcing Candidates through Various Channels

Screening and Interviewing Techniques

Building a Talent Pipeline

Chapter 7: Client Acquisition and Relationship Management

Identifying and Approaching Potential Clients

Pitching Your Services Effectively

Building Long-Term Client Relationships

Chapter 8: Operations and Workflow Management

Setting Up Efficient Workflow Processes

Implementing Technology Solutions

Managing Daily Operations and Staffing Assignments

Chapter 9: Financial Management and Profitability

How to start a staffing placement business

    Budgeting and Cash Flow Management

    Pricing Strategies and Negotiation Techniques

    Maximizing Profit Margins

Chapter 10: Scaling and Growth Strategies

    Expanding Your Service Offerings

    Diversifying into New Markets

    Strategic Partnerships and Alliances

Chapter 11: Managing Risks and Challenges

    Mitigating Legal and Compliance Risks

    Handling Cash Flow Challenges

    Dealing with Client and Candidate Issues

Chapter 12: Exit Strategies and Future Outlook

    Planning for Exit or Expansion

    Adapting to Industry Changes and Trends

    The Future of Staffing Placement Businesses

Conclusion

Appendix I: Sample Business Plan Template

Appendix II: Legal Checklist for Staffing Agencies

    Business Formation and Structure:

How to start a staffing placement business

Employment Laws and Regulations

Contract Management:

Regulatory Compliance

Data Protection and Privacy

Intellectual Property Protection

Compliance Monitoring and Training

Appendix III: Recruitment and Onboarding Templates

Appendix IV: Glossary of Terms

How to start a staffing placement business

Chapter 1: Introduction to Staffing Placement Business

Understanding the Staffing Industry

The staffing industry plays a crucial role in connecting businesses with qualified talent. It encompasses a wide range of services, including temporary staffing, permanent placement, and talent acquisition solutions. Staffing agencies act as intermediaries between employers and job seekers, facilitating the hiring process and ensuring a smooth transition for both parties. With the evolving nature of work and the increasing demand for specialized skills, the staffing industry has experienced significant growth in recent years. From entry-level positions to executive roles, staffing agencies cater to the diverse needs of businesses across various sectors.

One of the defining characteristics of the staffing industry is its flexibility. Companies often turn to staffing agencies to meet fluctuating demand, cover seasonal peaks, or fill temporary vacancies. This flexibility allows businesses to scale their workforce up or down as needed without the long-term commitment associated with traditional hiring. For job seekers, staffing agencies provide access to a wide range of opportunities, including temporary assignments, contract work, and direct placements. This diversity enables individuals to explore different industries, gain valuable experience, and advance their careers.

Another key aspect of the staffing industry is its role in addressing skills shortages and talent gaps. In today's competitive job market, employers face challenges in finding candidates with the right mix of skills, experience, and cultural fit. Staffing agencies help bridge this gap by leveraging their networks, expertise, and resources to source, screen, and place qualified candidates. Whether it's in-demand technical skills or specialized industry knowledge, staffing agencies play a vital role in matching employers with talent that meets their specific requirements.

Furthermore, the staffing industry is characterized by its dynamic nature and constant innovation. Technology plays a crucial role in streamlining processes, improving efficiency, and enhancing the candidate experience. From applicant tracking systems to online job boards and mobile recruiting apps, staffing agencies leverage a variety of tools and platforms to stay ahead of the curve. Additionally, emerging trends such as remote work, gig economy, and artificial intelligence continue to shape the future of the staffing industry, presenting both opportunities and challenges for businesses and job seekers alike.

Benefits and Challenges of Starting a Staffing Agency

Starting a staffing agency offers numerous benefits for aspiring entrepreneurs looking to enter the lucrative field of talent acquisition. One of the primary advantages is the low barrier to entry compared to other industries. With minimal upfront investment and relatively low overhead costs, individuals can launch a staffing agency with a modest budget and scalable business model. This accessibility makes it an attractive option for those seeking entrepreneurial freedom and flexibility without the need for significant capital or resources.

Another benefit of starting a staffing agency is the potential for high profitability and recurring revenue streams. As businesses increasingly rely on staffing agencies to meet their hiring needs, there is a growing demand for talent acquisition services across various industries and sectors. By building a strong client base and delivering exceptional value, staffing agencies can generate steady income through placement fees, contract commissions, and ongoing client relationships. This revenue stability provides a solid foundation for growth and expansion in the long term.

Additionally, starting a staffing agency allows individuals to make a meaningful impact on the lives of both employers and job seekers. By connecting companies with top talent and helping individuals secure

How to start a staffing placement business

rewarding opportunities, staffing agencies play a vital role in driving economic growth, promoting workforce development, and fostering career advancement. This sense of purpose and fulfillment can be immensely rewarding for entrepreneurs who are passionate about making a difference in their communities and industries.

However, despite its many benefits, starting a staffing agency also comes with its fair share of challenges and obstacles. One of the main challenges is building a reputable brand and establishing credibility in a competitive market. With numerous staffing agencies vying for clients and candidates, new entrants must differentiate themselves through superior service, innovative solutions, and a strong value proposition. This requires strategic planning, effective marketing, and consistent delivery of results to earn the trust and loyalty of stakeholders.

Another challenge faced by staffing agencies is navigating the complex legal and regulatory landscape governing the industry. From employment laws and regulations to licensing requirements and compliance standards, there are various legal considerations that must be addressed to operate a staffing agency legally and ethically. Failure to comply with these regulations can result in fines, penalties, and reputational damage, making it essential for entrepreneurs to stay informed and adhere to best practices in all aspects of their operations.

Furthermore, managing cash flow and financial stability can be a significant challenge for new staffing agencies, especially during the early stages of growth and expansion. Balancing expenses, securing funding, and managing payroll can strain resources and impact profitability if not handled effectively. This requires careful financial planning, budgeting, and risk management to ensure the long-term sustainability and success of the business. Despite these challenges, with the right strategy, mindset, and perseverance, aspiring entrepreneurs can overcome obstacles and build a thriving staffing agency that delivers value to clients and candidates alike.

Overview of the Recruitment Process

The recruitment process is a critical aspect of staffing agency operations, encompassing various stages from sourcing candidates to onboarding new hires. Understanding the key components of the recruitment process is essential for staffing agencies to attract top talent, meet client needs, and achieve successful placements. The process typically begins with a thorough assessment of client requirements, including job descriptions, qualifications, and cultural fit criteria.

Once client needs are identified, staffing agencies leverage a variety of sourcing methods to attract candidates, including job boards, social media, networking events, and employee referrals. These channels help casting a wide net to reach passive and active job seekers, ensuring a diverse pool of candidates with the skills and experience needed to excel in the role. Additionally, staffing agencies may utilize talent databases, applicant tracking systems, and other technology solutions to streamline the sourcing process and manage candidate pipelines effectively.

Once candidates are identified, the next step is to screen and evaluate their qualifications, experience, and suitability for the position. This involves conducting interviews, skills assessments, background checks, and reference checks to verify credentials and assess fit. Staffing agencies play a crucial role in vetting candidates and ensuring they meet client expectations in terms of skills, culture, and performance. By thoroughly evaluating candidates, staffing agencies can present the most qualified and suitable candidates to clients for consideration.

After candidates have been screened and selected, the recruitment process enters the placement phase, where candidates are presented to clients for review and consideration. Staffing agencies act as intermediaries, facilitating communication between clients and candidates, coordinating interviews, and negotiating job offers on behalf of both parties. This collaborative approach ensures a smooth and seamless transition for all stakeholders involved, from initial engagement to final placement.

Once a candidate has been selected and hired, the recruitment process transitions to the onboarding phase, where new hires are integrated into the client's organization and provided with the necessary training and support to succeed in their roles. Staffing agencies play a supportive role during the onboarding process, providing guidance, feedback, and assistance to both clients and candidates to ensure a positive experience and successful outcomes.

Therefore, the recruitment process is a multifaceted and dynamic process that requires careful planning, execution, and coordination to achieve successful outcomes. By understanding the various stages of the recruitment process and leveraging best practices and technology solutions, staffing agencies can effectively meet client needs, attract top talent, and drive positive outcomes for all stakeholders involved.

Chapter 2: Market Research and Analysis

Identifying Target Markets and Niches

Before launching a staffing agency, it's essential to conduct thorough market research to identify target markets and niches where the business can thrive. One approach to identifying target markets is to analyze industry trends, economic indicators, and demographic data to identify sectors experiencing growth or undergoing transformation. For example, industries such as healthcare, technology, and hospitality are known to have high demand for qualified talent and may present lucrative opportunities for staffing agencies. Additionally, it's important to consider geographic factors such as population density, employment rates, and local business ecosystems when identifying target markets. By focusing on specific industries or geographic regions, staffing agencies can tailor their services to meet the unique needs of clients and candidates in those areas.

In addition to identifying target markets, it's also important to identify niche markets or specialized areas where the staffing agency can differentiate itself and carve out a competitive advantage. Niche markets can include specific job roles, industries, or demographic segments that have unique staffing needs or require specialized expertise. For example, niche markets such as healthcare staffing, IT consulting, or executive search services may offer higher margins and lower competition compared to broader markets. By specializing in a niche market, staffing agencies can position themselves as experts in their field, attract higher-quality clients and candidates, and command premium pricing for their services.

Furthermore, when identifying target markets and niches, it's important to consider the long-term viability and growth potential of each opportunity. This involves analyzing market size, growth projections, competitive landscape, and barriers to entry to assess the attractiveness of different markets. For example, industries with high demand for skilled labor, low market saturation, and favorable regulatory environments may present greater growth opportunities for staffing agencies. By conducting thorough market research and analysis, staffing agencies can make informed decisions about where to focus their efforts and allocate resources to maximize growth and profitability.

Lastly, identifying target markets and niches also involves understanding the needs, preferences, and pain points of clients and candidates within those markets. This requires conducting surveys, interviews, and focus groups to gather feedback and insights from key stakeholders. By understanding the unique challenges and opportunities facing clients and candidates in target markets, staffing agencies can tailor their services, marketing messages, and value propositions to address specific needs and differentiate themselves from competitors. This customer-centric approach is essential for building strong relationships, driving customer loyalty, and achieving sustainable growth in the long term.

Analyzing Competitors and Industry Trends

In addition to identifying target markets and niches, analyzing competitors and industry trends is essential for positioning a staffing agency for success. Competitor analysis involves identifying and evaluating competing staffing agencies operating in the same target markets or serving similar niches. This includes researching their services, pricing strategies, customer segments, marketing tactics, and strengths and weaknesses to identify areas of opportunity and potential threats. By understanding the competitive landscape, staffing agencies can identify gaps in the market, differentiate themselves from competitors, and develop strategies to gain a competitive advantage.

Furthermore, analyzing industry trends is crucial for staying informed about market dynamics, emerging opportunities, and potential threats that may impact the staffing industry. This involves monitoring macroeconomic indicators, regulatory changes, technological advancements, and demographic shifts that may influence hiring trends and workforce dynamics. For example, trends such as remote work, gig economy, and artificial intelligence are reshaping the way companies recruit and manage talent, presenting both opportunities and challenges for staffing agencies. By staying abreast of industry trends, staffing agencies can anticipate market shifts, adapt their strategies accordingly, and capitalize on emerging opportunities to stay ahead of the competition.

Moreover, competitor analysis and industry trend analysis go hand in hand, as understanding how competitors are responding to industry trends can provide valuable insights into market dynamics and competitive positioning. For example, if competitors are investing heavily in technology solutions or expanding into new service lines, it may indicate a shift in client preferences or emerging opportunities that staffing agencies should be aware of. By benchmarking against competitors and learning from their successes and failures, staffing agencies can refine their strategies, innovate their services, and stay ahead of the curve in a rapidly evolving industry.

Additionally, competitor analysis and industry trend analysis can also uncover potential partnership opportunities, collaboration possibilities, and strategic alliances that can benefit staffing agencies. By identifying complementary businesses, vendors, or industry associations, staffing agencies can leverage existing networks and resources to expand their reach, access new markets, and offer additional value to clients and candidates. This collaborative approach can enhance competitiveness, drive innovation, and create win-win opportunities for all stakeholders involved.

Assessing Demand and Supply Dynamics

Assessing demand and supply dynamics is a critical aspect of market research and analysis for staffing agencies, as it directly impacts the availability of talent, client demand, and pricing dynamics. Demand refers to the number of job openings, hiring needs, and staffing requirements within target markets and industries, while supply refers to the pool of available candidates and talent available to fill those roles. By understanding the balance between demand and supply, staffing agencies can develop strategies to address talent shortages, meet client needs, and optimize their operations for maximum efficiency and profitability.

One approach to assessing demand and supply dynamics is to analyze labor market data, employment statistics, and hiring trends to identify areas of high demand and potential talent shortages. For example, industries such as healthcare, technology, and skilled trades may experience persistent shortages of qualified talent due to factors such as demographic trends, skill gaps, and competition for top talent. By focusing on industries with high demand and limited supply, staffing agencies can position themselves as strategic partners for clients seeking hard-to-fill positions and specialized skills.

Moreover, assessing demand and supply dynamics also involves understanding the preferences, motivations, and career aspirations of candidates within target markets and industries. This requires conducting surveys, interviews, and focus groups to gather insights into factors such as salary expectations, job preferences, work-life balance, and career advancement opportunities. By understanding what motivates candidates and drives their decision-making process, staffing agencies can tailor their recruitment strategies, compensation packages, and employee value propositions to attract and retain top talent.

Furthermore, assessing demand and supply dynamics also involves analyzing client needs, hiring patterns, and workforce planning strategies to anticipate future demand and align recruitment efforts accordingly. For example, industries such as hospitality, retail, and seasonal businesses may experience fluctuations in demand based on factors such as consumer spending, tourism trends, and seasonal peaks. By working closely with clients to understand their business objectives and staffing requirements, staffing agencies can proactively anticipate demand fluctuations, adjust their recruitment strategies, and provide value-added services to help clients meet their workforce needs.

Conclusively, assessing demand and supply dynamics also involves leveraging technology and data analytics to track market trends, monitor competitor activities, and identify emerging opportunities in real-time. By harnessing the power of big data, predictive analytics, and machine learning algorithms, staffing agencies can gain deeper insights into market dynamics, identify patterns and trends, and make data-driven decisions to stay ahead of the curve. This analytical approach enables staffing agencies to optimize their operations, allocate resources effectively, and capitalize on opportunities to grow their business and dominate the recruitment industry.

Chapter 3: Crafting Your Business Plan

Defining Your Business Model

Defining your business model is a crucial first step in starting a staffing agency as it lays the foundation for your operations, revenue streams, and value proposition. The staffing industry offers various business models, including temporary staffing, permanent placement, contract-to-hire, and executive search. Each model has its own advantages and considerations, so it's essential to choose one that aligns with your goals, resources, and target market. Temporary staffing involves placing workers on short-term assignments with client companies, while permanent placement focuses on recruiting candidates for full-time positions. Contract-to-hire allows clients to evaluate candidates on a temporary basis before offering them a permanent position, while executive search specializes in recruiting senior-level executives and top talent for leadership roles.

Once you've chosen a business model, the next step is to define your value proposition and differentiate yourself from competitors. This involves identifying your unique selling points, strengths, and competitive advantages that set you apart in the market. Whether it's your industry expertise, niche specialization, technology solutions, or customer service excellence, your value proposition should resonate with clients and candidates and address their pain points and needs. By clearly defining your value proposition, you can attract clients, candidates, and talent partners who align with your brand and value what you have to offer.

Moreover, defining your business model also involves establishing your pricing strategy and revenue model. This includes determining how you will generate revenue, whether through placement fees, hourly rates, or retainer agreements, and setting competitive pricing that reflects the value of your services and the market demand. Additionally, you'll need to consider factors such as billing cycles, payment terms, and discounts to ensure consistent cash flow and profitability. By aligning your pricing strategy with your value proposition and target market, you can position yourself competitively in the market while maximizing revenue and profitability.

Furthermore, defining your business model requires outlining your service offerings, processes, and delivery mechanisms to ensure consistency and quality in your operations. This includes developing standardized procedures for sourcing candidates, screening applicants, matching talent with client needs, and managing client relationships. Additionally, you'll need to invest in technology solutions such as applicant tracking systems, customer relationship management software, and online portals to streamline your operations, improve efficiency, and enhance the candidate and client experience. By defining your business model and operational framework, you can create a roadmap for success and lay the groundwork for building a scalable and sustainable staffing agency.

Setting Goals and Objectives

Setting goals and objectives is a critical aspect of crafting a business plan for a staffing agency as it provides a roadmap for success and helps measure progress and performance over time. When setting goals and objectives, it's essential to be specific, measurable, achievable, relevant, and time-bound (SMART) to ensure clarity and accountability. This involves defining both short-term and long-term goals that align with your vision, mission, and values and reflect the priorities and aspirations of your business.

One common goal for staffing agencies is to achieve revenue targets and profitability goals. This involves setting specific revenue targets for the first year, second year, and subsequent years of operation, as well as establishing profit margins and financial benchmarks to track performance and monitor profitability. Additionally, you may set goals for client acquisition, candidate placement, and market share growth to drive revenue and expand your client base over time. By setting ambitious yet achievable revenue goals, you can motivate your team, focus your efforts, and drive sustainable growth and success.

Moreover, setting goals and objectives also involves defining metrics and key performance indicators (KPIs) to track progress and measure success. This includes metrics such as client satisfaction scores, candidate retention rates, time-to-fill ratios, and revenue per placement to assess the effectiveness of your operations and identify areas for improvement. By regularly monitoring KPIs and performance metrics, you can identify trends, spot opportunities, and make data-driven decisions to optimize your business processes and achieve your goals.

Furthermore, setting goals and objectives requires aligning your business objectives with the needs and expectations of your stakeholders, including clients, candidates, employees, and investors. This involves identifying their priorities, concerns, and aspirations and incorporating them into your goal-setting process to ensure buy-in and support. For example, you may set goals for employee training and development, diversity and inclusion initiatives, or community outreach programs to enhance employee engagement, attract top talent, and strengthen your brand reputation. By aligning your goals with the interests of your stakeholders, you can build trust, foster collaboration, and create a shared sense of purpose and commitment to success.

Additionally, setting goals and objectives also involves establishing a timeline and action plan for achieving your goals. This includes breaking down larger goals into smaller, actionable steps, assigning responsibilities and deadlines, and regularly reviewing progress and adjusting strategies as needed. By taking a systematic and disciplined approach to goal setting and execution, you can stay focused, overcome obstacles, and achieve meaningful results that propel your business forward.

Financial Planning and Projections

Financial planning and projections are essential components of crafting a business plan for a staffing agency as they provide a roadmap for managing finances, allocating resources, and achieving profitability. Financial planning involves forecasting your income, expenses, and cash flow to ensure sufficient funding and resources to support your operations and growth objectives. This includes estimating startup costs, operating expenses, and revenue projections for the first year, second year, and subsequent years of operation, as well as identifying potential sources of funding and capital to finance your business.

One of the first steps in financial planning is to estimate your startup costs, including expenses such as office space, equipment, technology, licensing fees, insurance, and marketing and advertising expenses. By accurately estimating your startup costs, you can determine how much funding you'll need to launch and sustain your staffing agency until it becomes profitable. Additionally, you'll need to consider factors such as working capital, contingency reserves, and buffer funds to cover unexpected expenses and fluctuations in cash flow during the startup phase.

Moreover, financial planning also involves projecting your revenue and profit potential based on market research, industry trends, and competitive analysis. This includes estimating your average placement fees, bill rates, and gross margins, as well as forecasting your client acquisition rate, candidate placement rate, and revenue growth trajectory over time. Additionally, you'll need to factor in variables such as seasonality, economic cycles, and market volatility when projecting your financial performance to ensure accuracy and reliability in your projections.

Furthermore, financial planning requires developing a budget and expense plan to manage your cash flow and allocate resources effectively. This involves categorizing your expenses into fixed costs (e.g., rent, utilities, salaries) and variable costs (e.g., marketing, travel, training) and establishing spending limits and controls to prevent overspending and ensure financial stability. Additionally, you'll need to track your actual expenses against your budget and make adjustments as needed to stay on track and avoid financial surprises.

Additionally, financial planning also involves assessing your funding options and capital structure to finance your staffing agency's operations and growth initiatives. This may include self-funding using personal savings, loans, lines of credit, or seeking external financing from investors, venture capitalists, or business partners. By evaluating the pros and cons of each funding option and aligning your financing strategy with your business objectives and risk tolerance, you can secure the capital you need to launch and scale your staffing agency successfully.

To recapitulate, financial planning and projections are essential for crafting a comprehensive business plan for a staffing agency as they provide a roadmap for managing finances, allocating resources, and achieving profitability. By accurately estimating startup costs, projecting revenue and profit potential, developing a budget and expense plan, and assessing funding options, you can ensure the financial health and success of your staffing agency in the long term.

Chapter 4: Legal and Regulatory Compliance

Choosing the Right Legal Structure

Choosing the right legal structure is a critical decision when starting a staffing agency as it determines your business's tax obligations, liability protection, and operational flexibility. There are several legal structures to consider, including sole proprietorship, partnership, limited liability company (LLC), and corporation. Each structure has its own advantages and considerations, so it's essential to weigh the pros and cons carefully and choose the one that best aligns with your goals, risk tolerance, and long-term vision for your staffing agency.

One of the simplest and most common legal structures for small businesses is a sole proprietorship, where the business is owned and operated by a single individual. Sole proprietorships offer simplicity, flexibility, and minimal paperwork requirements, making them an attractive option for solo entrepreneurs and freelancers looking to start a staffing agency on a smaller scale. However, sole proprietorships provide no liability protection, meaning the owner is personally responsible for any debts, liabilities, or legal claims against the business, putting their personal assets at risk.

Another option is a partnership, where two or more individuals join forces to start and run a staffing agency together. Partnerships can be general partnerships, where all partners share equally in the profits and liabilities, or limited partnerships, where some partners have limited liability and are not actively involved in the day-to-day operations of the business. While partnerships offer shared decision-making, resources, and expertise, they also come with the risk of conflicts, disagreements, and shared liability among partners, making clear agreements and communication essential for success.

Additionally, a limited liability company (LLC) is a popular choice for staffing agencies due to its combination of liability protection and operational flexibility. LLCs provide owners with limited liability, meaning their personal assets are protected from business debts and legal claims, while also offering pass-through taxation, where profits and losses are reported on the owners' individual tax returns. Furthermore, LLCs offer flexibility in management structure, ownership, and profit distribution, making them an ideal choice for small to medium-sized staffing agencies looking for a balance of liability protection and operational flexibility.

Lastly, a corporation is a separate legal entity that offers the highest level of liability protection but also comes with greater administrative complexity and tax obligations. Corporations can be either C corporations or S corporations, each with its own tax treatment and ownership requirements. While corporations offer strong liability protection and flexibility in ownership and fundraising, they require formalities such as regular meetings, record-keeping, and compliance with corporate governance regulations, making them better suited for larger staffing agencies with complex ownership structures and significant growth ambitions.

Ultimately, the right legal structure for your staffing agency will depend on factors such as your risk tolerance, tax considerations, ownership structure, and growth aspirations. By carefully evaluating your options and consulting with legal and financial professionals, you can choose the legal structure that best meets your needs and positions your staffing agency for long-term success and growth.

Licensing and Permits

Licensing and permits are essential for operating a staffing agency legally and ethically, as they ensure compliance with state and local regulations, protect the interests of clients and candidates, and uphold industry standards and best practices. The specific licensing and permit requirements for staffing agencies vary depending on factors such as location, business model, and industry specialization, so it's essential to research and understand the requirements in your jurisdiction before launching your agency.

One of the most important licenses for staffing agencies is a business license or permit, which is required to operate legally in most jurisdictions. Business licenses are typically issued by local governments and may vary depending on factors such as business type, location, and industry. Additionally, staffing agencies may need to obtain industry-specific licenses or permits, such as employment agency licenses, professional licenses for recruiters or HR professionals, or special permits for industries such as healthcare or transportation.

Furthermore, staffing agencies may need to register with state labor departments or employment agencies and comply with regulations governing the operation of staffing firms, including advertising and marketing practices, fee structures, and candidate screening and placement procedures. Additionally, staffing agencies may be subject to regulations such as the Fair Labor Standards Act (FLSA), which sets standards for minimum wage, overtime pay, and child labor, and the Equal Employment Opportunity (EEO) laws, which prohibit discrimination based on race, color, religion, sex, national origin, age, disability, or genetic information.

Moreover, licensing and permit requirements for staffing agencies may also include bonding and insurance requirements to protect clients, candidates, and employees from financial loss or liability. Surety bonds are often required as a form of financial guarantee to ensure that staffing agencies comply with state regulations and fulfill their obligations to clients and candidates. Additionally, staffing agencies may need to obtain insurance coverage such as general liability insurance, professional liability insurance, and workers' compensation insurance to protect against claims and lawsuits arising from negligence, errors, or accidents.

Lastly, staffing agencies should stay informed about changes to licensing and permit requirements, as regulations may evolve over time in response to industry trends, technological advancements, and changes in labor laws. By staying proactive and maintaining compliance with licensing and permit requirements, staffing agencies can protect their reputation, mitigate risks, and build trust with clients, candidates, and regulatory authorities.

Compliance with Employment Laws and Regulations

Compliance with employment laws and regulations is a top priority for staffing agencies, as failure to adhere to legal requirements can result in fines, penalties, lawsuits, and reputational damage. Staffing agencies are subject to a wide range of federal, state, and local laws governing employment practices, wage and hour standards, workplace safety, and anti-discrimination and harassment protections, so it's essential to stay informed and ensure compliance in all aspects of your operations.

One of the most critical areas of compliance for staffing agencies is ensuring fair and lawful employment practices, including compliance with anti-discrimination and equal employment opportunity (EEO) laws. These laws prohibit discrimination based on race, color, religion, sex, national origin, age, disability, or genetic information in hiring, promotion, compensation, and other employment decisions. Staffing agencies must ensure that their recruiting, screening, and hiring practices are free from bias and comply with EEO laws to protect the rights and dignity of all candidates and employees.

Moreover, staffing agencies must comply with wage and hour laws, including the Fair Labor Standards Act (FLSA), which sets standards for minimum wage, overtime pay, recordkeeping, and child labor. Staffing agencies must ensure that all employees are paid at least the minimum wage and receive overtime pay for hours worked beyond 40 hours per week, as required by law. Additionally, staffing agencies must maintain accurate records of hours worked, wages earned, and deductions taken to demonstrate compliance with wage and hour laws.

Furthermore, staffing agencies must comply with workplace safety regulations to ensure the health and safety of their employees and clients. This includes providing a safe work environment, conducting risk assessments, implementing safety protocols and procedures, and providing training and education on workplace hazards and safety practices. Additionally, staffing agencies may need to comply with industry-specific safety regulations, such as those governing construction sites, healthcare facilities, or transportation operations, to protect employees from workplace injuries and accidents.

Additionally, staffing agencies must comply with tax laws and regulations governing payroll taxes, employee classification, and reporting requirements. This includes withholding and remitting payroll taxes, issuing W-2 forms to employees, and filing quarterly and annual tax returns with the appropriate taxing authorities. Additionally, staffing agencies must accurately classify employees as either employees or independent contractors based on IRS guidelines and ensure compliance with tax and labor laws governing employee benefits, insurance coverage, and worker classification.

Therefore, compliance with employment laws and regulations is a critical responsibility for staffing agencies, as it ensures fair treatment of employees, protects the rights of candidates and clients, and upholds industry standards and best practices. By staying informed about legal requirements, implementing robust compliance programs, and conducting regular audits and reviews, staffing agencies can mitigate risks, maintain trust and credibility, and build a solid foundation for long-term success and growth.

Chapter 5: Building Your Brand

Building a strong brand is essential for the success of any staffing agency, as it helps differentiate your business from competitors, attract clients and candidates, and establish trust and credibility in the marketplace. Therefore, this chapter explores key strategies for building your brand, including developing a unique value proposition, creating a compelling brand identity, and establishing an online presence to reach your target audience effectively.

Developing a Unique Value Proposition

Your value proposition is the promise of value that you deliver to your clients and candidates, and it's essential to develop a unique value proposition that sets you apart from competitors and resonates with your target audience. To develop a unique value proposition, start by identifying the needs, pain points, and preferences of your clients and candidates and determining how your staffing agency can address them in a way that competitors cannot.

One approach to developing a unique value proposition is to focus on a specific niche or industry where you have expertise or experience and tailor your services to meet the unique needs of clients and candidates in that niche. For example, if you have experience in healthcare staffing, you could position your agency as a specialist in healthcare recruitment, offering specialized expertise, networks, and resources that generalist agencies cannot match.

Additionally, consider what sets your staffing agency apart from competitors, whether it's your industry knowledge, technology solutions, customer service, or track record of success. Your unique value proposition should highlight these strengths and communicate the benefits of working with your agency in a clear and compelling way. For example, if your agency offers a faster time-to-fill or a higher placement success rate than competitors, emphasize these advantages in your value proposition to attract clients and candidates seeking results.

Moreover, involve your team in the process of developing your unique value proposition, as they can provide valuable insights and perspectives based on their experience and expertise. By involving your team in the process, you can ensure buy-in and alignment with your brand messaging and empower them to communicate your value proposition effectively to clients and candidates in their interactions.

Lastly, regularly review and refine your unique value proposition based on feedback from clients, candidates, and employees, as well as changes in market dynamics, industry trends, and competitive landscape. By continuously evolving and adapting your value proposition to meet the evolving needs of your target audience, you can stay relevant, competitive, and compelling in the marketplace.

Creating a Compelling Brand Identity

Your brand identity is the visual and emotional representation of your staffing agency, including your logo, colors, typography, imagery, messaging, and tone of voice. Creating a compelling brand identity is essential for building brand recognition, fostering trust and credibility, and creating a memorable impression with clients and candidates. Here are key steps to creating a compelling brand identity for your staffing agency:

Start by defining your brand personality and values, including the characteristics, traits, and attributes that you want your brand to embody. Consider what sets your staffing agency apart and how you want to be perceived by clients, candidates, and stakeholders. Your brand personality should be authentic, consistent, and aligned with your unique value proposition and target audience.

Next, develop visual elements that reflect your brand personality and values, including your logo, colors, typography, and imagery. Your logo is the centerpiece of your brand identity and should be simple, memorable, and versatile, representing your agency's identity and values. Choose colors and typography that reflect your brand personality and evoke the emotions and feelings you want to convey to your audience. Additionally, select imagery that resonates with your target audience and reinforces your brand messaging and positioning.

Moreover, create brand messaging that communicates your unique value proposition, benefits, and personality in a clear and compelling way. Your brand messaging should be consistent across all touchpoints, including your website, social media profiles, marketing materials, and client and candidate communications. Use language that resonates with your target audience and reinforces your brand values and positioning, whether it's professional, friendly, authoritative, or innovative.

Additionally, ensure consistency in your brand identity across all touchpoints and channels to build brand recognition and trust with your audience. This includes maintaining consistency in your logo usage, colors, typography, imagery, and messaging across your website, social media profiles, email communications, and print materials. Consistency helps reinforce your brand identity and creates a cohesive and memorable experience for clients and candidates.

Lastly, regularly evaluate and refine your brand identity based on feedback from clients, candidates, and stakeholders, as well as changes in market dynamics, industry trends, and competitive landscape. Your brand identity should evolve and adapt over time to stay relevant, resonate with your target audience, and differentiate your staffing agency in the marketplace.

Establishing an Online Presence

In today's digital age, having a strong online presence is essential for reaching your target audience, building brand awareness, and attracting clients and candidates to your staffing agency. Here are key strategies for establishing an effective online presence for your staffing agency:

Create a professional website that showcases your brand identity, services, and value proposition in a clear and compelling way. Your website should be user-friendly, mobile-responsive, and easy to navigate, with intuitive navigation, engaging content, and clear calls-to-action to encourage visitors to contact you or learn more about your services. Additionally, optimize your website for search engines (SEO) to improve visibility and attract organic traffic from potential clients and candidates searching for staffing services online.

Moreover, leverage social media platforms such as LinkedIn, Facebook, Twitter, and Instagram to engage with your target audience, share valuable content, and build relationships with clients, candidates, and industry influencers. Post regularly on social media to stay top-of-mind with your audience and share industry insights, job opportunities, success stories, and company updates to showcase your expertise and credibility in the recruitment industry. Additionally, participate in relevant industry groups and forums to network with peers, share best practices, and stay informed about industry trends and developments.

Furthermore, invest in online advertising and marketing strategies such as pay-per-click (PPC) advertising, social media ads, and content marketing to reach a wider audience and drive traffic to your website. Target your ads to specific demographics, industries, or geographic regions to maximize relevance and effectiveness, and track key metrics such as click-through rates, conversion rates, and return on investment (ROI) to measure the success of your campaigns and optimize your marketing efforts over time.

Additionally, leverage content marketing to position your staffing agency as a thought leader and trusted resource in the recruitment industry. Create and share high-quality content such as blog posts, articles, whitepapers, case studies, and videos that address common pain points, challenges, and trends facing clients and candidates in your target market. By providing valuable insights and information, you can attract and engage your target audience, build credibility and trust, and drive inbound leads and inquiries to your agency.

Lastly, monitor and manage your online reputation and reviews to ensure a positive perception of your staffing agency among clients, candidates, and stakeholders. Respond promptly to feedback, both positive and negative, and take proactive steps to address any issues or concerns raised by clients or candidates. By actively managing your online reputation, you can build trust, credibility, and goodwill with your audience and differentiate your staffing agency from competitors in the marketplace.

Chapter 6: Recruitment and Talent Acquisition

Recruitment and talent acquisition are at the core of a staffing agency's operations, as they involve sourcing, screening, and selecting qualified candidates to meet the needs of clients. Hence, it is essential to understand the key strategies and techniques for effectively recruiting and acquiring top talent, including sourcing candidates through various channels, screening and interviewing techniques, and building a talent pipeline to ensure a steady supply of qualified candidates for clients.

Sourcing Candidates through Various Channels

Sourcing candidates through various channels is essential for building a diverse and qualified talent pool to meet the needs of clients across industries and job functions. There are several channels and methods for sourcing candidates, including online job boards, social media platforms, networking events, referrals, and direct sourcing. Here are some key strategies for sourcing candidates through various channels:

1. Online Job Boards: Online job boards such as Indeed, LinkedIn, Glassdoor, and Monster are popular platforms for posting job openings and attracting candidates. These platforms allow staffing agencies to reach a wide audience of job seekers and advertise job opportunities to attract qualified candidates. Additionally, many job boards offer advanced search and filtering options to help recruiters narrow down their candidate search based on criteria such as skills, experience, location, and industry.

2. Social Media Platforms: Social media platforms such as LinkedIn, Facebook, Twitter, and Instagram are valuable tools for sourcing candidates and building relationships with potential candidates. Staffing agencies can leverage social media to share job openings, engage with candidates, and showcase their employer brand and company culture. Additionally, social media platforms offer networking opportunities to connect with passive candidates and tap into hidden talent pools.

3. Networking Events: Networking events such as job fairs, industry conferences, career expos, and professional association meetings are excellent opportunities for staffing agencies to meet potential candidates and build relationships with industry professionals. By attending networking events, recruiters can expand their network, learn about industry trends and developments, and identify top talent in their field.

4. Referrals: Employee referrals are a powerful source of candidate referrals, as employees are often well-connected within their industry and can recommend qualified candidates for open positions. Staffing agencies can incentivize employee referrals through referral programs and rewards to encourage employees to refer qualified candidates from their professional networks.

5. Direct Sourcing: Direct sourcing involves proactively reaching out to potential candidates who may not be actively searching for jobs but possess the skills and experience desired by clients. Staffing agencies can use techniques such as targeted email campaigns, cold calling, and personalized outreach to engage passive candidates and generate interest in job opportunities.

Leveraging a combination of these sourcing channels and methods gives staffing agencies the ability cast a wide net and attract a diverse pool of candidates to meet the needs of clients and fill open positions effectively.

Screening and Interviewing Techniques

Screening and interviewing techniques are critical for assessing candidate qualifications, skills, and fit for specific job roles and client requirements. Effective screening and interviewing techniques help staffing agencies identify top talent, ensure candidate quality, and streamline the hiring process. Here are some key techniques for screening and interviewing candidates:

1. Resume Screening: Resume screening involves reviewing candidate resumes to assess their qualifications, skills, experience, and suitability for specific job roles. Staffing agencies can use applicant tracking systems (ATS) to automate the resume screening process and filter resumes based on predefined criteria such as keywords, experience level, and education. Additionally, recruiters can use screening questions and assessments to further evaluate candidate qualifications and fit for client requirements.

2. Phone Screening: Phone screening is an initial step in the recruitment process where recruiters conduct brief phone interviews with candidates to assess their communication skills, interest in the position, and alignment with client requirements. Phone screening allows recruiters to quickly identify promising candidates and determine if they meet the basic qualifications and criteria for the position before moving forward with in-person interviews.

3. Behavioral Interviews: Behavioral interviews are structured interviews that focus on assessing candidate behavior, skills, and competencies based on past experiences and situations. During a behavioral interview, recruiters ask candidates to provide specific examples of how they've demonstrated key skills and competencies relevant to the job role, such as teamwork, problem-solving, and decision-making. Behavioral interviews help recruiters assess candidate fit for specific job requirements and client expectations.

4. Technical Assessments: Technical assessments are used to evaluate candidates' technical skills, knowledge, and proficiency in specific areas relevant to the job role, such as programming languages, software applications, or industry-specific tools and technologies. Technical assessments may include written tests, coding exercises, case studies, or practical assignments to assess candidates' abilities and ensure they possess the required technical competencies for the position.

5. Cultural Fit Interviews: Cultural fit interviews assess candidates' alignment with the company culture, values, and work environment to ensure they will thrive and succeed in the organization. Recruiters use cultural fit interviews to evaluate candidates' personality, communication style, work ethic, and compatibility with the company culture and team dynamics. Cultural fit interviews help ensure a harmonious and productive work environment and reduce the risk of turnover and cultural misalignment.

By employing a combination of these screening and interviewing techniques, staffing agencies can effectively assess candidate qualifications, skills, and fit for specific job roles and client requirements, ensuring a successful match between candidates and clients.

Building a Talent Pipeline

Building a talent pipeline is essential for ensuring a steady supply of qualified candidates to meet the needs of clients and fill open positions quickly and efficiently.

A talent pipeline is a pool of candidates who have been identified, engaged, and nurtured over time, allowing staffing agencies to tap into a network of qualified talent whenever a job opening arises. Here are some key strategies for building a talent pipeline:

1. Proactive Candidate Sourcing: Proactive candidate sourcing involves continuously identifying and engaging potential candidates who may be a good fit for future job opportunities. Staffing agencies can use sourcing channels such as online job boards, social media, networking events, and employee referrals to build a pipeline of qualified candidates with diverse skills and backgrounds.

2. Talent Relationship Management: Talent relationship management (TRM) involves building and maintaining relationships with candidates over time to keep them engaged, informed, and interested in future job opportunities. TRM includes regular communication, networking events, personalized outreach, and providing value-added services such as career coaching, resume review, and professional development opportunities to candidates.

3. Candidate Engagement Strategies: Candidate engagement strategies are designed to keep candidates interested and invested in the staffing agency and its job opportunities. This may include sending regular email newsletters, hosting webinars and workshops, providing industry insights and career advice, and offering exclusive access to job openings and networking events. By providing value-added content and services, staffing agencies can keep candidates engaged and motivated to pursue opportunities with their agency.

4. Talent Pool Segmentation: Talent pool segmentation involves categorizing candidates into different segments based on factors such as skills, experience, industry, location, and job preferences. By segmenting their talent pool, staffing agencies can tailor their communications and outreach efforts to specific candidate groups and personalize their messaging to address their unique needs and interests.

5. Succession Planning: Succession planning involves identifying high-potential candidates within the talent pipeline and grooming them for future leadership roles within the organization. Staffing agencies can provide mentorship, training, and development opportunities to high-potential candidates to help them grow and advance in their careers while ensuring a pipeline of future leaders and top talent for the organization.

By implementing these strategies and techniques for building a talent pipeline, staffing agencies can ensure a steady supply of qualified candidates to meet the needs of clients, reduce time-to-fill for open positions, and gain a competitive advantage in the recruitment industry.

Chapter 7: Client Acquisition and Relationship Management

Client acquisition and relationship management are pivotal components of a successful staffing agency's operations. Building strong relationships with clients not only helps secure business but also fosters long-term partnerships that can lead to repeat business and referrals. In this chapter, we'll delve into strategies for identifying and approaching potential clients, pitching your services effectively, and building long-term client relationships to drive growth and success for your staffing agency.

Identifying and Approaching Potential Clients

Identifying and approaching potential clients is the first step in acquiring new business for your staffing agency. It involves researching industries and companies that may require staffing services and initiating contact to introduce your agency's offerings. Here are some strategies for identifying and approaching potential clients:

1. Market Research: Conduct thorough market research to identify industries and sectors with a high demand for staffing services. Look for industries experiencing growth or undergoing transformation, as they are likely to have a need for temporary or permanent staffing solutions. Additionally, research companies within these industries to understand their hiring needs, pain points, and priorities.

2. Networking: Networking is a valuable tool for connecting with potential clients and building relationships that can lead to business opportunities. Attend industry events, conferences, and networking functions to meet hiring managers, HR professionals, and decision-makers within target companies. Join industry associations and online forums to expand your network and stay informed about industry trends and developments.

3. Referrals: Leverage your existing client relationships and professional network to generate referrals for new business. Ask satisfied clients for referrals and recommendations, and offer incentives or rewards for referrals that result in new business. Additionally, reach out to industry partners, vendors, and service providers who may be able to refer clients to your agency.

4. Cold Outreach: Cold outreach involves reaching out to potential clients directly via email, phone, or social media to introduce your agency's services and explore opportunities for collaboration. Craft personalized messages tailored to each prospect's industry, company size, and specific hiring needs to demonstrate your understanding of their business and how your agency can add value.

Pitching Your Services Effectively

Pitching your services effectively is essential for persuading potential clients to choose your staffing agency over competitors. A compelling pitch should clearly communicate the value proposition of your agency and how your services can address the client's hiring needs and challenges. Here are some tips for pitching your services effectively:

1. Research: Before pitching to a potential client, conduct thorough research to understand their industry, company culture, hiring needs, and pain points. Tailor your pitch to address specific challenges or gaps in their workforce and demonstrate how your agency's services can provide solutions and deliver results.

2. Value Proposition: Clearly articulate your agency's value proposition and unique selling points that set you apart from competitors. Highlight your agency's expertise, industry knowledge, track record of success, and any specialized services or technology solutions that differentiate you from other staffing firms.

3. Customization: Customize your pitch to resonate with each potential client's needs and priorities.

Demonstrate your understanding of their business and hiring requirements and propose tailored solutions that address their specific challenges and objectives. Personalize your pitch to show that you've done your homework and are genuinely invested in helping them achieve their goals.

4. Case Studies and Testimonials: Use case studies, success stories, and client testimonials to provide evidence of your agency's capabilities and results. Share examples of past projects or placements that demonstrate your ability to deliver quality candidates, reduce time-to-fill, and drive business outcomes for clients. Social proof can help build credibility and trust with potential clients.

By crafting a compelling pitch that demonstrates your agency's value proposition, customization, and track record of success, you can effectively persuade potential clients to choose your staffing agency for their hiring needs.

Building Long-Term Client Relationships

Building long-term client relationships is crucial for sustaining and growing your staffing agency's business over time. Long-term clients not only provide a steady stream of revenue but also become advocates for your agency and a source of referrals. Here are some strategies for building and nurturing long-term client relationships:

1. Communication: Maintain open and transparent communication with clients throughout the engagement process. Keep clients informed about candidate progress, feedback, and any updates or changes to the hiring process. Regularly check in with clients to gather feedback, address concerns, and ensure satisfaction with your agency's services.

2. Responsiveness: Be responsive and proactive in addressing client inquiries, requests, and concerns. Respond promptly to client emails, phone calls, and messages, and follow up on any outstanding issues or action items. Anticipate client needs and take proactive steps to exceed their expectations and demonstrate your commitment to their success.

3. Value-Added Services: Offer value-added services and resources to help clients streamline their hiring processes, improve candidate quality, and achieve their business objectives. This may include providing industry insights and market trends, conducting salary benchmarking or talent assessments, or offering training and development programs for client staff.

4. Relationship Building: Invest time and effort in building personal relationships with key stakeholders and decision-makers within client organizations. Schedule regular meetings or check-ins to discuss ongoing projects, review performance metrics, and brainstorm strategies for future collaboration. Building rapport and trust with clients can lead to long-term partnerships and repeat business.

How to start a staffing placement business

Focusing on communication, responsiveness, value-added services, and relationship building, aids your ability to cultivate strong and lasting relationships with clients that contribute to the long-term success and growth of your staffing agency.

Chapter 8: Operations and Workflow Management

Setting Up Efficient Workflow Processes

Efficient workflow processes are the backbone of any successful staffing agency, ensuring that operations run smoothly, tasks are completed in a timely manner, and client and candidate needs are met effectively. Setting up efficient workflow processes involves defining clear procedures, automating repetitive tasks, and optimizing resource allocation to maximize productivity and minimize errors. Here are some key considerations for setting up efficient workflow processes:

1. Define Standard Operating Procedures (SOPs): Start by documenting standard operating procedures (SOPs) for key operational tasks and workflows, including candidate sourcing, screening, placement, client communication, and administrative tasks. SOPs provide a clear roadmap for employees to follow, ensure consistency and quality in service delivery, and facilitate training and onboarding of new staff members.

2. Streamline Workflows: Analyze existing workflows and identify opportunities to streamline processes and eliminate inefficiencies. Look for tasks that can be automated or simplified using technology solutions, such as applicant tracking systems (ATS), email templates, scheduling tools, and workflow automation software. Streamlining workflows helps reduce manual workloads, minimize errors, and improve overall efficiency and productivity.

3. Establish Clear Communication Channels: Effective communication is essential for smooth workflow management, especially in a fast-paced environment like a staffing agency. Establish clear communication channels and protocols for internal communication among team members, as well as external communication with clients, candidates, and stakeholders. Use collaboration tools such as project management software, instant messaging platforms, and video conferencing tools to facilitate communication and collaboration among remote teams.

4. Implement Quality Control Measures: Implement quality control measures to ensure consistency and accuracy in service delivery and minimize errors or discrepancies. This may include regular audits and reviews of workflow processes, performance metrics and KPIs to monitor productivity and quality standards, and feedback mechanisms to gather input from clients, candidates, and employees for continuous improvement.

Defining clear SOPs, streamlining workflows, establishing communication channels, and implementing quality control measures facilitates staffing agencies to set up efficient workflow processes that drive operational excellence and support business growth and success.

Implementing Technology Solutions

Technology plays a crucial role in streamlining operations and improving efficiency in staffing agencies. Implementing technology solutions can help automate repetitive tasks, streamline workflows, enhance communication and collaboration, and provide valuable insights and analytics for data-driven decision-making. Here are some key technology solutions to consider for staffing agencies:

1. Applicant Tracking Systems (ATS): An ATS is a software platform that automates the recruitment process, from sourcing and screening candidates to tracking applications and managing candidate data. ATS solutions help streamline workflow processes, improve candidate management and engagement, and enhance collaboration among recruiters and hiring managers. Features may include resume parsing, candidate tracking, job posting, interview scheduling, and reporting and analytics.

2. Customer Relationship Management (CRM) Software: CRM software helps staffing agencies manage client relationships and sales pipelines, track client interactions, and automate sales and marketing activities. CRM solutions provide a centralized database for storing client contacts, communication history, and sales opportunities, allowing recruiters to track client preferences, follow up on leads, and nurture relationships for long-term success.

3. Communication and Collaboration Tools: Communication and collaboration tools such as email, instant messaging, video conferencing, and project management software are essential for facilitating communication and collaboration among internal teams, remote workers, clients, and candidates. These tools enable real-time communication, file sharing, task management, and project collaboration, enhancing productivity and efficiency in a distributed work environment.

4. Analytics and Reporting Tools: Analytics and reporting tools provide valuable insights and metrics for tracking key performance indicators (KPIs), measuring operational efficiency, and identifying areas for improvement. Analytics dashboards and reports can help staffing agencies monitor metrics such as time-to-fill, candidate quality, client satisfaction, and revenue growth, allowing them to make data-driven decisions and optimize workflow processes for better outcomes.

Managing Daily Operations and Staffing Assignments

Effective management of daily operations and staffing assignments is essential for meeting client needs, fulfilling job orders, and ensuring smooth workflow processes. Managing daily operations involves overseeing tasks such as candidate sourcing, screening, placement, client communication, and administrative duties, while managing staffing assignments requires matching qualified candidates with client job requirements and ensuring successful placements. Here are some strategies for managing daily operations and staffing assignments effectively:

1. Prioritize Tasks and Assignments: Prioritize tasks and assignments based on urgency, client priorities, and revenue impact to ensure that critical tasks are completed first and client needs are met in a timely manner. Use task management tools and calendars to schedule and track assignments, set deadlines, and allocate resources effectively to maximize productivity and minimize bottlenecks.

2. Monitor Workload and Capacity: Monitor employee workload and capacity to ensure that staffing levels are sufficient to meet client demand and workload fluctuations. Use workload management tools and capacity planning techniques to assess resource availability, identify potential bottlenecks or overloads, and redistribute workloads as needed to maintain productivity and quality standards.

3. Foster Collaboration and Teamwork: Foster a culture of collaboration and teamwork among employees to encourage knowledge sharing, peer support, and cross-functional collaboration. Encourage open communication, regular team meetings, and brainstorming sessions to facilitate idea exchange, problem-solving, and innovation. By working together as a cohesive team, employees can overcome challenges more effectively and achieve better results for clients and candidates.

4. Provide Training and Development: Invest in training and development programs to equip employees with the skills, knowledge, and tools they need to perform their jobs effectively and advance in their careers. Offer training on software applications, industry best practices, customer service skills, and compliance requirements to ensure that employees are equipped to meet client needs and deliver high-quality service.

Therefore, by prioritizing tasks, monitoring workload and capacity, fostering collaboration and teamwork, and providing training and development opportunities, staffing agencies can effectively manage daily operations and staffing assignments to meet client needs and drive business success.

Chapter 9: Financial Management and Profitability

Effective financial management involves managing budgets, cash flow, pricing strategies, and profit margins to ensure profitability and long-term growth. Therefore, it is crucial to understand the key aspects of financial management for staffing agencies, including budgeting and cash flow management, pricing strategies and negotiation techniques, and maximizing profit margins to drive business success.

Budgeting and Cash Flow Management

Budgeting involves forecasting revenue and expenses, setting financial goals, and allocating resources effectively to achieve profitability and growth. Cash flow management involves monitoring cash inflows and outflows, managing working capital, and ensuring that the agency has sufficient funds to cover expenses and obligations. Here are some key considerations for budgeting and cash flow management:

1. Forecasting Revenue and Expenses: Start by forecasting revenue and expenses based on historical data, market trends, and projected growth. Identify sources of revenue, such as client placements, temporary staffing contracts, and additional services or upsells. Estimate expenses, including salaries and benefits, marketing and advertising, technology infrastructure, office rent, and administrative overhead. Use financial forecasting techniques such as trend analysis, regression analysis, and scenario planning to anticipate potential fluctuations and uncertainties in revenue and expenses.

2. Setting Financial Goals: Set clear financial goals and objectives for your staffing agency, such as revenue targets, profit margins, and growth milestones. Break down long-term goals into shorter-term objectives and develop actionable strategies and tactics to achieve them. Monitor progress regularly against financial targets and adjust strategies as needed to stay on track and address any deviations or challenges.

3. Allocating Resources Effectively: Allocate resources effectively to optimize efficiency and maximize return on investment (ROI). Prioritize investments in areas that drive revenue growth, such as sales and marketing, technology infrastructure, and talent acquisition. Balance short-term expenses with long-term investments in strategic initiatives that support business growth and sustainability. Monitor resource allocation to ensure that funds are allocated appropriately to support key priorities and minimize waste or inefficiency.

4. Managing Cash Flow: Manage cash flow effectively to ensure that the agency has sufficient liquidity to meet financial obligations and seize opportunities for growth. Monitor cash inflows and outflows closely, including client payments, payroll, vendor invoices, and other expenses. Implement cash flow forecasting tools and techniques to predict cash flow fluctuations and identify potential cash shortfalls or surpluses. Maintain a cash reserve or line of credit to cover unexpected expenses or temporary cash flow gaps and avoid relying on short-term borrowing or high-interest loans.

Pricing Strategies and Negotiation Techniques

Pricing strategies and negotiation techniques play a critical role in determining the profitability and competitiveness of a staffing agency. Setting the right pricing structure and effectively negotiating rates with clients and candidates can impact revenue, profit margins, and overall business success. Here are some key considerations for pricing strategies and negotiation techniques:

1. Value-Based Pricing: Adopt a value-based pricing approach that aligns pricing with the perceived value of your services to clients. Instead of pricing based solely on costs or market rates, focus on the value proposition of your agency, including factors such as industry expertise, candidate quality, speed of placement, and customer service. Emphasize the benefits and outcomes that clients can expect from working with your agency and justify your pricing based on the value you deliver.

2. Flexible Pricing Models: Offer flexible pricing models that cater to the diverse needs and budgets of clients. Consider offering tiered pricing packages with different service levels and pricing tiers based on client requirements, volume of placements, or duration of contracts. Provide options for hourly, daily, or project-based pricing for temporary staffing assignments, as well as contingency or retained search fees for permanent placements. Flexibility in pricing allows you to accommodate different client preferences and maximize revenue opportunities.

3. Negotiation Skills: Develop strong negotiation skills to effectively negotiate rates and terms with clients and candidates. Prepare thoroughly for negotiations by researching market rates, understanding client needs and priorities, and identifying potential areas for compromise or concession. Focus on building rapport and trust with clients, listening actively to their concerns, and positioning your agency as a valuable partner who is committed to delivering results. Be prepared to walk away from negotiations if the terms are not favorable or do not align with your agency's financial objectives.

4. Value-Added Services: Differentiate your agency and justify higher pricing by offering value-added services that enhance the client experience and deliver additional value. This may include additional recruitment services such as candidate assessments, background checks, skills testing, onboarding support, and training programs. Highlight the benefits of these value-added services and how they contribute to client satisfaction, employee retention, and overall business success.

Maximizing Profit Margins

Maximizing profit margins is essential for achieving financial sustainability and long-term growth in a staffing agency. Profit margins represent the difference between revenue and expenses and are a key indicator of business profitability and efficiency. By focusing on strategies to increase revenue, reduce costs, and improve operational efficiency, staffing agencies can maximize profit margins and drive business success. Here are some strategies for maximizing profit margins:

1. Increase Revenue Streams: Diversify revenue streams to reduce reliance on any single source of income and create multiple streams of revenue. In addition to traditional staffing services, explore opportunities to offer additional services or upsells such as training and development programs, consulting services, recruitment process outsourcing (RPO), and managed services solutions. Identify niche markets or specialized industries where your agency can provide value-added services and command higher rates.

2. Control Costs: Control costs and expenses to improve profit margins and operational efficiency. Review expenses regularly and identify areas where costs can be reduced or eliminated without sacrificing quality or service delivery. Look for opportunities to streamline processes, negotiate better terms with vendors and suppliers, and leverage economies of scale to lower costs. Implement cost-saving initiatives such as remote work arrangements, energy efficiency measures, and technology investments that improve productivity and reduce overhead expenses.

3. Monitor Key Performance Indicators (KPIs): Monitor key performance indicators (KPIs) related to revenue, expenses, and profitability to track business performance and identify areas for improvement. Key financial metrics to track may include gross margin, net profit margin, bill rate, pay rate, fill rate, and average placement fee. Analyze KPI trends over time, benchmark against industry standards, and set targets for improvement to drive profitability and financial success.

4. Optimize Operational Efficiency: Optimize operational efficiency to reduce waste, minimize inefficiencies, and improve productivity throughout the organization. Streamline workflow processes, automate repetitive tasks, and leverage technology solutions to increase efficiency and reduce manual workloads. Invest in employee training and development to enhance skills and competencies, empower employees to take ownership of their work, and foster a culture of continuous improvement and innovation.

Chapter 10: Scaling and Growth Strategies

Scaling and growth are essential for a staffing agency to expand its reach, increase revenue, and achieve long-term success in the competitive recruitment industry. This chapter will explore strategies for scaling and growing a staffing business, including expanding service offerings, diversifying into new markets, and forming strategic partnerships and alliances to drive growth and expansion.

Expanding Your Service Offerings

Expanding service offerings is a key strategy for scaling and growing a staffing agency. By diversifying the types of services provided, agencies can attract new clients, increase revenue streams, and meet the evolving needs of the market. Here are some ways to expand your service offerings:

How to start a staffing placement business

1. Temporary Staffing: If your agency primarily focuses on permanent placements, consider expanding into temporary staffing to cater to clients who require short-term or project-based staffing solutions. Temporary staffing can include providing contract employees, seasonal workers, or temporary-to-hire placements to meet fluctuating demand or project-based needs.

2. Specialized Recruitment Services: Identify niche markets or specialized industries where there is a high demand for skilled talent and offer specialized recruitment services to cater to those sectors. This may include providing executive search services, technical recruiting, healthcare staffing, IT consulting, or other specialized services tailored to specific industries or job functions.

3. Recruitment Process Outsourcing (RPO): Offer recruitment process outsourcing (RPO) services to clients who prefer to outsource all or part of their recruitment process to an external provider. RPO solutions involve managing the end-to-end recruitment process on behalf of the client, from sourcing and screening candidates to onboarding and managing talent pools. RPO can help clients reduce hiring costs, improve time-to-fill, and access specialized expertise and resources.

4. Additional HR Services: Expand beyond traditional staffing services and offer additional HR-related services to clients, such as workforce planning, talent management, employee training and development, HR consulting, and compliance assistance. By providing comprehensive HR solutions, agencies can position themselves as strategic partners to clients and add value beyond just staffing placements.

Diversifying into New Markets

Diversifying into new markets is another effective strategy for scaling and growing a staffing agency. By expanding into new geographic regions or industry sectors, agencies can access untapped opportunities, reduce dependency on a single market, and mitigate risk. Here are some ways to diversify into new markets:

1. Geographic Expansion: Consider expanding into new geographic markets by opening branch offices or satellite locations in strategic locations. Research potential markets to identify regions with high demand for staffing services, favorable business climates, and growth opportunities. Develop a market entry strategy, including market research, competitive analysis, and local networking and marketing efforts to establish a presence and attract clients and candidates.

2. Industry Verticals: Diversify into new industry verticals or sectors where there is demand for staffing services and specialized expertise. Research industries that are experiencing growth or undergoing transformation and align your service offerings with their hiring needs. Develop industry-specific marketing and sales strategies to target key decision-makers and establish credibility within targeted verticals.

3. Target New Client Segments: Identify new client segments or customer demographics that could benefit from your staffing services. This may include targeting small businesses, startups, government agencies, nonprofit organizations, or specific demographic groups such as millennials, women-owned businesses, or minority-owned enterprises. Tailor your marketing messaging and value proposition to resonate with the needs and priorities of these target segments.

4. Explore Niche Markets: Explore niche markets or emerging sectors where there is a demand for specialized talent or services. This could include niche industries such as renewable energy, biotechnology, e-commerce, or emerging technologies like artificial intelligence, blockchain, or virtual reality. Position your agency as a specialist in these niche markets and develop expertise and networks to capitalize on growth opportunities.

Strategic Partnerships and Alliances

Forming strategic partnerships and alliances can accelerate growth and expansion for staffing agencies by leveraging complementary resources, expertise, and networks. Strategic partnerships enable agencies to access new markets, expand service offerings, and enhance competitive advantage. Here are some strategies for forming strategic partnerships and alliances:

1. Industry Associations: Join industry associations, trade organizations, and networking groups within the staffing and recruitment industry to connect with peers, share best practices, and access industry insights and resources. Participate in industry events, conferences, and webinars to build relationships and identify potential collaboration opportunities with other agencies, vendors, and service providers.

2. Vendor Partnerships: Form partnerships with vendors and technology providers that offer complementary products or services to support your staffing operations. This may include partnering with software vendors for applicant tracking systems (ATS), background screening services, payroll processing, or compliance management solutions. Collaborate with vendors to integrate systems, streamline workflows, and enhance operational efficiency.

3. Client Referral Partnerships: Develop referral partnerships with clients, consultants, and other professionals who may refer business to your agency. Offer incentives or rewards for client referrals that result in new business opportunities, such as discounts on future services or gift cards. Cultivate relationships with key referral partners and provide excellent service to encourage repeat referrals and ongoing collaboration.

4. Strategic Alliances: Form strategic alliances with other staffing agencies or service providers to pool resources, share leads, and collaborate on larger projects or contracts. Identify agencies or partners with complementary strengths, expertise, or geographic coverage and explore opportunities for joint ventures, co-marketing initiatives, or subcontracting arrangements. By combining forces, agencies can access new markets, win larger contracts, and compete more effectively against larger competitors.

Undoubtedly, scaling and growing a staffing agency requires a strategic approach to expanding service offerings, diversifying into new markets, and forming strategic partnerships and alliances. By leveraging these growth strategies, agencies can access new opportunities, increase market share, and position themselves for sustained success and profitability in the evolving recruitment landscape.

Chapter 11: Managing Risks and Challenges

Managing risks and challenges is an integral part of running a staffing business. From legal and compliance issues to cash flow challenges and client and candidate issues, staffing agencies must be prepared to navigate various obstacles to ensure smooth operations and long-term success. Understanding the strategies for mitigating legal and compliance risks, handling cash flow challenges, and dealing with client and candidate issues effectively are crucial in order to manage risks and challenges.

Mitigating Legal and Compliance Risks

Staffing agencies operate in a highly regulated environment, and compliance with legal requirements is crucial to avoid costly penalties, lawsuits, and damage to reputation. Mitigating legal and compliance risks requires a proactive approach to staying informed about relevant laws and regulations, implementing robust policies and procedures, and conducting regular audits to ensure compliance. Here are some strategies for mitigating legal and compliance risks:

1. Stay Informed: Stay abreast of changes in employment laws, regulations, and industry standards that may impact your staffing business. Subscribe to legal newsletters, attend industry conferences and seminars, and consult with legal experts to stay informed about emerging issues and best practices. Develop a comprehensive understanding of key areas such as employment discrimination, wage and hour laws, worker classification, background checks, and data privacy regulations.

2. Implement Policies and Procedures: Develop and implement clear and comprehensive policies and procedures to ensure compliance with legal and regulatory requirements. This may include policies related to equal employment opportunity (EEO), anti-discrimination and harassment, employee classification, wage and hour laws, safety and health regulations, background screening, and data protection. Communicate policies to employees through training programs, employee handbooks, and regular updates to ensure understanding and compliance.

3. Conduct Regular Audits: Conduct regular internal audits and reviews of your staffing operations to identify and address compliance issues proactively. Review key areas such as employee records, payroll practices, candidate screening processes, client contracts, and data security protocols. Identify areas of non-compliance or potential risk and take corrective action to address deficiencies, strengthen controls, and mitigate future risks.

4. Seek Legal Advice: Consult with legal counsel or HR professionals with expertise in employment law and staffing industry regulations to seek guidance on compliance matters, interpret legal requirements, and mitigate risks effectively. Build a relationship with a trusted legal advisor who understands your business and industry-specific challenges and can provide timely advice and representation in legal matters.

Handling Cash Flow Challenges

Cash flow challenges are a common concern for staffing agencies, especially those that rely on invoicing clients for payment after placing candidates. Delayed payments, seasonal fluctuations in demand, and unexpected expenses can impact cash flow and strain financial resources. Effectively managing cash flow requires careful planning, monitoring, and proactive measures to maintain liquidity and financial stability. Here are some strategies for handling cash flow challenges:

1. Forecast Cash Flow: Develop a cash flow forecast to project future inflows and outflows of cash based on anticipated revenue and expenses. Estimate cash receipts from client payments, track outstanding invoices, and forecast expenses such as payroll, rent, utilities, and other overhead costs. Update the cash flow forecast regularly to reflect changes in business conditions and adjust strategies accordingly.

2. Accelerate Cash Collections: Take steps to accelerate cash collections and reduce the time between invoicing clients and receiving payment. Implement efficient invoicing processes, including timely and accurate invoicing, clear payment terms, and follow-up procedures for overdue invoices. Offer incentives for early payment or consider offering discounts for prompt payment to encourage clients to pay invoices more quickly.

3. Negotiate Payment Terms: Negotiate favorable payment terms with clients to improve cash flow and reduce the risk of late payments. Seek shorter payment terms, such as net 15 or net 30 days, and clarify payment terms upfront in client contracts to avoid misunderstandings or disputes. Consider requiring upfront deposits or retainer fees for new clients or high-risk accounts to secure payment and mitigate credit risk.

4. Manage Expenses: Manage expenses prudently to conserve cash and maintain adequate liquidity during periods of cash flow challenges. Review expenses regularly and identify opportunities to reduce costs or defer discretionary spending until cash flow improves. Consider renegotiating contracts with vendors or suppliers for better terms or discounts, and prioritize essential expenses to ensure business continuity.

Dealing with Client and Candidate Issues

Client and candidate issues can arise unexpectedly and have a significant impact on the reputation and success of a staffing agency. Whether it's a client dispute, candidate complaint, or performance issue, handling these issues promptly and professionally is essential to maintaining positive relationships and preserving business credibility. Here are some strategies for dealing with client and candidate issues effectively:

1. Communicate Openly: Foster open and transparent communication with clients and candidates to address issues promptly and resolve conflicts amicably. Encourage feedback from clients and candidates about their experiences and concerns and listen attentively to their feedback. Respond promptly to inquiries, address issues with empathy and professionalism, and keep stakeholders informed throughout the resolution process.

2. Address Concerns Proactively: Anticipate potential issues and address concerns proactively before they escalate into larger problems. Monitor client and candidate satisfaction regularly through surveys, feedback forms, and performance reviews. Identify patterns or trends in feedback and take corrective action to address underlying issues or improve service delivery. By demonstrating a proactive approach to problem-solving, agencies can build trust and credibility with clients and candidates.

3. Provide Exceptional Service: Deliver exceptional service to clients and candidates to exceed expectations and mitigate potential issues. Focus on understanding and meeting the needs of clients and candidates, delivering high-quality placements, and providing ongoing support and follow-up throughout the engagement. Anticipate potential challenges or obstacles and take proactive steps to address them before they impact the client or candidate experience.

4. Resolve Disputes Fairly: Handle client disputes and candidate complaints fairly and impartially, following established protocols and procedures for conflict resolution. Investigate complaints thoroughly, gather relevant information and evidence, and work collaboratively with all parties involved to find a resolution that is satisfactory to everyone. Document all communications and resolutions to ensure transparency and accountability.

Therefore, managing risks and challenges is an ongoing responsibility for staffing agencies, requiring proactive measures and strategic approaches to mitigate legal and compliance risks, handle cash flow challenges, and address client and candidate issues effectively. By implementing these strategies, staffing agencies can protect their business, maintain financial stability, and build lasting relationships with clients and candidates in the competitive recruitment industry.

Chapter 12: Exit Strategies and Future Outlook

Exit strategies and future outlook are crucial considerations for staffing business owners looking to plan for the long-term success and sustainability of their enterprises. Whether preparing for exit or expansion, adapting to industry changes and trends, or envisioning the future of staffing businesses, strategic foresight and planning are essential. To wrap up this book, we will explore various aspects of exit strategies and future outlook for staffing businesses, including planning for exit or expansion, adapting to industry changes and trends, and the future landscape of the staffing industry.

Planning for Exit or Expansion

Planning for exit or expansion is a pivotal decision for staffing business owners, whether they are considering selling their business, passing it on to successors, or scaling up operations. Exit strategies allow owners to realize the value of their investment and transition to the next phase of their professional or personal journey, while expansion strategies enable growth and diversification to capture new opportunities. Here are some considerations for planning exit or expansion:

1. Evaluate Business Objectives: Start by evaluating your business objectives and personal goals to determine whether an exit or expansion strategy aligns with your long-term vision. Consider factors such as financial goals, lifestyle preferences, retirement plans, and legacy considerations. Determine whether you are seeking an exit to cash out and retire, pass the business on to family members or successors, or pursue growth and expansion opportunities to maximize value and market share.

2. Assess Market Conditions: Assess market conditions and industry trends to gauge the feasibility and timing of an exit or expansion strategy. Evaluate factors such as market demand, competition, economic conditions, and regulatory changes that may impact the valuation and attractiveness of your business. Consult with industry experts, financial advisors, and business brokers to gain insights into market dynamics and identify opportune moments to execute your chosen strategy.

3. Explore Exit Options: Explore various exit options available to staffing business owners, such as selling the business outright, merging with a strategic partner or competitor, or transitioning ownership to family members or employees through a management buyout or employee stock ownership plan (ESOP). Evaluate the pros and cons of each option in terms of financial returns, tax implications, continuity of operations, and personal preferences. Seek professional advice from legal, financial, and tax advisors to navigate the complexities of the exit process and maximize value.

4. Develop a Growth Strategy: If pursuing expansion, develop a growth strategy that aligns with your business objectives and market opportunities. Identify growth drivers such as geographic expansion, diversification of service offerings, acquisition of competitors or complementary businesses, or strategic partnerships and alliances. Develop a detailed business plan and financial projections to support your growth strategy and secure financing or investment capital as needed to fund expansion initiatives.

Adapting to Industry Changes and Trends

The staffing industry is constantly evolving, driven by technological advancements, demographic shifts, regulatory changes, and shifting market dynamics. To remain competitive and relevant, staffing businesses must adapt to industry changes and trends proactively. This requires staying informed about emerging trends, investing in innovation and technology, and adopting agile business practices. Here are some ways staffing businesses can adapt to industry changes:

1. Embrace Technology: Embrace technology as a driver of innovation and efficiency in staffing operations. Invest in applicant tracking systems (ATS), customer relationship management (CRM) software, artificial intelligence (AI) tools, and automation technologies to streamline recruitment processes, improve candidate sourcing and screening, and enhance client engagement. Leverage data analytics and predictive modeling to identify trends, optimize decision-making, and drive business growth.

2. Focus on Candidate Experience: Prioritize candidate experience as a competitive differentiator in a talent-driven market. Enhance the recruitment process by providing personalized, seamless, and transparent experiences for candidates, from initial application to onboarding and beyond. Leverage technology to create interactive job portals, mobile-friendly applications, and virtual interviewing platforms that make it easy for candidates to engage with your agency and find their ideal job opportunities.

3. Adapt to Remote Work Trends: Adapt to the growing trend of remote work and flexible work arrangements by expanding your talent pool beyond geographic boundaries. Embrace virtual recruiting and remote hiring practices to connect with top talent regardless of location and cater to the evolving preferences of candidates and clients for remote work options. Invest in virtual collaboration tools, video conferencing platforms, and remote onboarding processes to support remote work arrangements effectively.

4. Address Compliance and Diversity: Stay abreast of regulatory changes and compliance requirements related to employment law, data privacy, and diversity and inclusion. Ensure that your staffing practices comply with legal and ethical standards and promote diversity, equity, and inclusion in hiring and workplace practices. Develop diversity initiatives, training programs, and diversity sourcing strategies to attract and retain a diverse talent pool and meet the evolving needs of clients and candidates.

The Future of Staffing Placement Businesses

The future of staffing placement businesses is shaped by emerging trends, disruptive technologies, and evolving workforce dynamics that will redefine the way staffing services are delivered and consumed. To thrive in the future landscape, staffing businesses must anticipate future trends, innovate continuously, and evolve their business models to stay ahead of the curve. Here are some future scenarios and trends shaping the future of staffing businesses:

1. Gig Economy and Freelancing: The rise of the gig economy and freelancing will continue to reshape the nature of work, with more workers opting for flexible, project-based engagements over traditional employment arrangements. Staffing businesses will need to adapt to this trend by offering flexible staffing solutions, facilitating gig work opportunities, and engaging with independent contractors and freelancers to meet client demands for contingent talent.

2. Skills-Based Hiring: Skills-based hiring will become increasingly important as employers prioritize candidates with the right skills and competencies to fill specific roles, regardless of traditional credentials or qualifications. Staffing businesses will need to focus on assessing and validating candidates' skills, providing training and upskilling programs to bridge skills gaps, and offering talent solutions that align with clients' evolving skill requirements.

3. AI and Automation: Advances in artificial intelligence (AI) and automation will revolutionize staffing processes, from candidate sourcing and screening to job matching and onboarding. Staffing businesses will leverage AI-powered tools and algorithms to streamline recruitment workflows, improve candidate matching accuracy, and deliver personalized experiences for clients and candidates. Human recruiters will increasingly focus on high-touch, value-added activities such as relationship-building, negotiation, and strategic consulting.

4. Talent Marketplaces and Platforms: Talent marketplaces and digital platforms will emerge as key players in the staffing ecosystem, connecting employers with a global talent pool and offering on-demand access to specialized skills and expertise. Staffing businesses will need to adapt to this shift by embracing digital platforms, participating in talent marketplaces, and offering innovative staffing solutions that leverage the power of technology to match talent with opportunities effectively.

Conclusion

Starting and managing a staffing placement business requires careful planning, strategic execution, and a commitment to excellence. Throughout this comprehensive guide, we have explored every aspect of launching, growing, and managing a lucrative staffing agency, from understanding the industry landscape to implementing proven growth hacks. Now, as we conclude our journey, let's reflect on the key takeaways and insights gained from this ultimate guide to entrepreneurial freedom in the recruitment industry.

First and foremost, we emphasized the importance of understanding the staffing industry and its dynamics. By familiarizing yourself with the intricacies of recruitment, including market trends, client needs, and candidate preferences, you can position your agency for success from the outset. Recognizing the benefits and challenges of starting a staffing agency is essential for making informed decisions and navigating potential obstacles along the way. From the outset, aspiring entrepreneurs must grasp the fundamentals of the recruitment process, from sourcing candidates to making placements, to establish a strong foundation for their business.

Crafting a comprehensive business plan is the next critical step in launching a staffing agency. Defining your business model, setting clear goals and objectives, and developing robust financial projections are essential elements of a successful business plan. Financial planning, in particular, plays a crucial role in ensuring the viability and sustainability of your agency, from budgeting and cash flow management to pricing strategies and profitability analysis. By meticulously planning every aspect of your business, you can minimize risks and maximize opportunities for growth and profitability.

Legal and regulatory compliance is another paramount consideration for staffing business owners. Choosing the right legal structure, obtaining necessary licenses and permits, and ensuring compliance with employment laws and regulations are fundamental to protecting your business and mitigating legal risks. By prioritizing compliance from the outset, you can build a reputation for integrity and trustworthiness while avoiding costly penalties and legal disputes that could jeopardize your agency's success.

Building a strong brand is essential for standing out in the competitive staffing industry. Developing a unique value proposition, creating a compelling brand identity, and establishing a robust online presence are key components of effective branding strategies. By differentiating your agency and communicating your value to clients and candidates, you can attract top talent, win new business, and build long-term relationships with clients and candidates alike.

Recruitment and talent acquisition are at the core of every staffing agency's operations. Sourcing candidates through various channels, employing screening and interviewing techniques, and building a talent pipeline are essential for meeting client needs and delivering exceptional service. By adopting innovative recruitment strategies and leveraging technology to streamline processes, you can enhance efficiency, quality, and speed in sourcing and placing candidates, gaining a competitive edge in the market.

Client acquisition and relationship management are critical for sustaining and growing your staffing business. Identifying and approaching potential clients, pitching your services effectively, and building long-term relationships are essential for winning new business and securing repeat business from satisfied clients. By delivering value, exceeding expectations, and fostering trust and loyalty, you can cultivate a loyal client base and drive sustainable growth for your agency.

Operations and workflow management are essential for ensuring smooth and efficient business operations. Setting up efficient workflow processes, implementing technology solutions, and managing daily operations and staffing assignments are crucial for optimizing productivity, quality, and performance. By leveraging technology to automate repetitive tasks, streamline workflows, and improve communication and collaboration, you can maximize efficiency and scalability while minimizing operational costs and errors.

Financial management and profitability are key priorities for every staffing agency. Budgeting and cash flow management, pricing strategies and negotiation techniques, and maximizing profit margins are essential for achieving financial success and sustainability. By closely monitoring financial performance, analyzing key metrics, and making data-driven decisions, you can optimize revenue, control costs, and maximize profitability to fuel growth and expansion.

Scaling and growth strategies are vital for taking your staffing business to the next level. Expanding service offerings, diversifying into new markets, and forming strategic partnerships and alliances are effective strategies for accelerating growth and expanding market reach. By seizing opportunities for expansion, innovating continuously, and adapting to evolving market trends, you can position your agency for long-term success and dominance in the recruitment industry.

Managing risks and challenges is an ongoing responsibility for staffing business owners. Mitigating legal and compliance risks, handling cash flow challenges, and dealing with client and candidate issues require a proactive approach and effective risk management strategies. By staying informed, implementing robust processes, and addressing issues promptly and professionally, you can protect your business, maintain client trust, and sustain growth in a dynamic and competitive environment.

Exit strategies and future outlook are crucial considerations for planning the long-term trajectory of your staffing business. Whether preparing for exit or expansion, adapting to industry changes and trends, or envisioning the future of staffing businesses, strategic foresight and planning are essential. By planning for exit or expansion, adapting to industry changes, and anticipating future trends, you can navigate the complexities of the industry and position your agency for sustained success and relevance in the years to come.

In conclusion, launching, growing, and managing a successful staffing agency requires vision, determination, and strategic execution. By following the comprehensive guide outlined in this book, aspiring entrepreneurs can embark on their entrepreneurial journey with confidence, equipped with the knowledge, insights, and tools needed to thrive in the competitive recruitment industry. Whether you are a seasoned industry professional or a novice entrepreneur, this ultimate guide to entrepreneurial freedom offers invaluable guidance and inspiration for building a lucrative staffing agency and dominating the recruitment industry with proven growth hacks.

How to start a staffing placement business

How to start a staffing placement business

How to start a staffing placement business

Appendix I: Sample Business Plan Template

This section provides a comprehensive sample business plan template for aspiring entrepreneurs looking to start a staffing agency. A well-crafted business plan serves as a roadmap for success, outlining the vision, goals, strategies, and operational details of the business. By following this sample template and customizing it to fit your specific needs and objectives, you can create a solid foundation for launching and growing a lucrative staffing agency.

1. Executive Summary:

The executive summary provides an overview of the staffing agency, highlighting its mission, vision, key objectives, and unique value proposition. It outlines the market opportunity, target market, competitive landscape, and growth strategy. The executive summary should be concise yet compelling, capturing the reader's attention and setting the stage for the rest of the business plan.

2. Company Description:

The company description provides detailed information about the staffing agency, including its history, ownership structure, legal status, and location. It describes the agency's core values, culture, and brand identity, as well as its unique selling proposition and competitive advantages. The company description also highlights the agency's target market segments, industry focus, and service offerings.

3. Market Analysis:

The market analysis section examines the staffing industry landscape, including market size, growth trends, and key drivers. It identifies target market segments and niche opportunities within the industry, as well as competitive dynamics and market positioning. The market analysis also assesses customer needs, preferences, and pain points, providing insights into market demand and opportunities for differentiation.

4. Organization and Management:

The organization and management section outlines the staffing agency's organizational structure, leadership team, and key personnel. It provides biographies of the founders and key executives, highlighting their relevant experience, expertise, and qualifications. The section also defines roles and responsibilities within the organization, including staffing, operations, sales, marketing, finance, and administration.

5. Service Offering:

The service offering section details the staffing agency's core services, including temporary staffing, permanent placement, executive search, and other specialized staffing solutions. It describes the agency's recruitment process, candidate sourcing strategies, screening and assessment methods, and placement services. The section also highlights any value-added services, such as training, onboarding, and workforce management solutions.

6. Marketing and Sales Strategy:

The marketing and sales strategy outlines how the staffing agency will attract clients and candidates, generate leads, and convert prospects into customers. It identifies target client industries and segments, as well as key decision-makers and influencers. The strategy includes a mix of marketing tactics, such as digital marketing, content marketing, social media, networking, events, and direct sales. It also defines sales processes, goals, metrics, and performance targets.

7. Financial Plan:

The financial plan presents the staffing agency's financial projections, including revenue forecasts, expense estimates, and cash flow projections. It outlines startup costs, operating expenses, and revenue sources, as well as funding requirements and sources of financing. The financial plan includes income statements, balance sheets, and cash flow statements for the first three to five years of operations, along with key assumptions and sensitivity analyses.

8. Operational Plan:

The operational plan details the staffing agency's day-to-day operations, including staffing processes, technology infrastructure, and administrative systems. It describes staffing workflows, candidate sourcing and screening procedures, client engagement processes, and employee onboarding and training protocols. The operational plan also addresses regulatory compliance, risk management, and quality assurance measures.

9. Risk Management:

The risk management section identifies potential risks and challenges facing the staffing agency and outlines strategies for mitigating and managing them effectively. It assesses legal and regulatory risks, market risks, financial risks, operational risks, and reputational risks. The section includes contingency plans, insurance coverage, and crisis management protocols to minimize the impact of adverse events on the agency's operations and reputation.

10. Appendices:

The appendices contain supplemental information and supporting documents, such as resumes of key personnel, market research data, industry reports, legal documents, and financial projections. They provide additional context and detail to support the main sections of the business plan and enhance the reader's understanding of the staffing agency's business model and growth potential.

By following this comprehensive sample business plan template, aspiring entrepreneurs can create a detailed roadmap for launching and growing a successful staffing agency. Customizing the template to fit your specific business goals, market dynamics, and operational requirements will help you build a solid foundation for entrepreneurial success in the competitive recruitment industry.

Appendix II: Legal Checklist for Staffing Agencies

Starting a staffing agency involves navigating a complex legal landscape to ensure compliance with various laws and regulations governing the recruitment and employment industry. From business formation to contract management, staffing agencies must adhere to legal requirements to protect their business interests and mitigate risks. In this chapter, we'll provide a comprehensive legal checklist for staffing agencies to help you stay compliant and operate your business successfully.

Business Formation and Structure:

1. Choose a Legal Structure: Determine the most suitable legal structure for your staffing agency, such as a sole proprietorship, partnership, limited liability company (LLC), or corporation. Consider factors such as liability protection, tax implications, and administrative requirements when selecting a legal structure.

2. Register Your Business: Register your staffing agency with the appropriate state and local authorities, obtaining any necessary business licenses and permits to operate legally. Ensure compliance with local zoning laws and regulations governing home-based businesses or office locations.

3. Obtain Employer Identification Number (EIN): Apply for an Employer Identification Number (EIN) from the Internal Revenue Service (IRS) to identify your staffing agency for tax purposes. An EIN is required for hiring employees, opening bank accounts, and filing tax returns.

Employment Laws and Regulations

4. Compliance with Labor Laws: Familiarize yourself with federal, state, and local labor laws governing employment practices, including minimum wage, overtime pay, employee classification (e.g., exempt vs. non-exempt), and anti-discrimination laws.

5. Worker Classification: Understand the distinction between employees and independent contractors and ensure proper classification to comply with tax and labor laws. Misclassification of workers can lead to legal liabilities, fines, and penalties.

6. Fair Labor Standards Act (FLSA) Compliance: Ensure compliance with the Fair Labor Standards Act (FLSA) regulations regarding minimum wage, overtime pay, recordkeeping, and child labor provisions. Implement policies and procedures to track employee work hours accurately and pay overtime when required.

7. Anti-Discrimination and Equal Employment Opportunity (EEO) Compliance: Adhere to anti-discrimination laws, including Title VII of the Civil Rights Act, the Americans with Disabilities Act (ADA), and the Age Discrimination in Employment Act (ADEA). Avoid discriminatory practices in hiring, promotion, and termination based on protected characteristics such as race, gender, age, disability, religion, or national origin.

Contract Management:

8. Client Contracts: Draft and review client contracts carefully to outline the terms and conditions of your staffing services, including rates, payment terms, liability, confidentiality, and dispute resolution mechanisms. Seek legal counsel to ensure contracts are legally enforceable and protect your agency's interests.

9. Candidate Agreements: Prepare candidate agreements or employment contracts to formalize the relationship between your agency and temporary employees or placements. Include terms related to job assignments, compensation, benefits, termination, and confidentiality to clarify rights and obligations.

10. Non-Disclosure and Non-Compete Agreements: Implement non-disclosure agreements (NDAs) to protect confidential information shared with clients, candidates, and employees. Consider non-compete agreements to prevent employees or contractors from competing with your agency or soliciting clients or candidates after leaving the company.

Regulatory Compliance

11. Health and Safety Regulations: Ensure compliance with occupational health and safety regulations to provide a safe work environment for employees and temporary workers. Implement workplace safety policies, conduct risk assessments, and provide training on safety protocols and emergency procedures.

12. Workers' Compensation Insurance: Obtain workers' compensation insurance coverage to protect employees and temporary workers in the event of work-related injuries or illnesses. Comply with state laws requiring employers to provide compensation benefits and medical care for injured workers.

13. Unemployment Insurance: Register for unemployment insurance coverage with the state workforce agency to provide benefits to eligible employees who lose their jobs through no fault of their own. Pay unemployment taxes and report wages as required by state unemployment insurance laws.

Data Protection and Privacy

14. Data Security and Privacy: Implement data security measures to safeguard sensitive information collected from clients, candidates, and employees. Comply with data protection laws such as the General Data Protection Regulation (GDPR) and the California Consumer Privacy Act (CCPA) by obtaining consent, protecting data integrity, and disclosing data practices.

15. Confidentiality Policies: Establish confidentiality policies and procedures to protect client and candidate information from unauthorized access, disclosure, or misuse. Train employees on data privacy best practices and enforce strict confidentiality protocols to maintain trust and integrity.

Intellectual Property Protection

16. Trademark Registration: Protect your staffing agency's brand identity by registering trademarks for company names, logos, and slogans with the United States Patent and Trademark Office (USPTO). Trademark registration provides legal rights to exclusive use and prevents others from using similar marks in the recruitment industry.

17. Copyright Protection: Secure copyrights for original content, marketing materials, website content, and training materials produced by your staffing agency. Copyright registration provides legal protection against unauthorized use, reproduction, or distribution of copyrighted works.

Compliance Monitoring and Training

18. Compliance Monitoring: Establish a compliance monitoring program to track regulatory changes, assess compliance risks, and ensure ongoing adherence to legal requirements. Conduct regular audits, reviews, and assessments of policies, procedures, and practices to identify areas for improvement and mitigate potential liabilities.

19. Employee Training: Provide comprehensive training and education to employees, recruiters, and managers on relevant laws, regulations, and ethical standards governing the staffing industry. Offer training modules on topics such as anti-discrimination, harassment prevention, data privacy, and ethical recruitment practices to promote legal compliance and ethical conduct.

By following this legal checklist for staffing agencies and consulting with legal professionals, you can ensure compliance with legal requirements and mitigate risks associated with operating in the recruitment industry. Prioritize legal compliance as a cornerstone of your business strategy to protect your agency's reputation, assets, and long-term success in the competitive staffing market.

Appendix III: Recruitment and Onboarding Templates

This section provides comprehensive templates for recruitment and onboarding, including job descriptions, interview questions, offer letters, and onboarding checklists, to help staffing agencies streamline their hiring processes and maximize candidate satisfaction.

1. Job Description Template:

Title: [Position Title]

Location: [Location]

Reports To: [Supervisor/Manager]

Company Overview:
[Provide a brief overview of the staffing agency, its mission, values, and culture]

Position Summary:

[Summarize the role and responsibilities of the position, including key duties, tasks, and objectives]

Key Responsibilities:

- [List the main responsibilities and duties of the position, including specific tasks and deliverables]
- [Provide details on required qualifications, skills, and experience]

Qualifications:

- [Education level]
- [Years of experience]
- [Skills and competencies]
- [Certifications or licenses]

Additional Requirements:

- [Physical requirements]
- [Travel requirements]
- [Work schedule]

2. Interview Question Template:

How to start a staffing placement business

1. Can you tell us about your relevant experience in [industry/field]?

2. What motivated you to apply for this position with our staffing agency?

3. How do you approach [specific task or challenge related to the role]?

4. Can you provide an example of a successful placement you facilitated in the past?

5. How do you prioritize tasks and manage deadlines in a fast-paced environment?

6. What strategies do you use to source and attract top talent?

7. How do you assess candidates' skills, qualifications, and cultural fit for a job opportunity?

8. How do you handle candidate objections or concerns during the recruitment process?

9. Can you describe a time when you faced a difficult client or candidate situation and how you resolved it?

10. What are your long-term career goals, and how do you see yourself contributing to our staffing agency's success?

3. Offer Letter Template:

[Staffing Agency Logo]

[Date]

[Candidate Name]
[Address]
[City, State, Zip Code]

Dear [Candidate Name],

We are pleased to offer you the position of [Position Title] at [Staffing Agency Name]. We believe that your skills, experience, and qualifications make you an excellent fit for this role, and we are excited to welcome you to our team.

Position Title: [Position Title]
Location: [Location]
Start Date: [Start Date]

Employment Type: [Full-Time/ Part-Time/ Temporary/ Contract]
Salary: [Salary Offer]
Benefits: [List of Benefits, if applicable]

As an employee of [Staffing Agency Name], you will be responsible for [Brief Description of Responsibilities]. Your contributions will play a key role in helping our clients meet their staffing needs and achieve their business objectives.

Please review the enclosed employment agreement, which outlines the terms and conditions of your employment, including compensation, benefits, confidentiality, and termination provisions. If you have any questions or require clarification on any aspect of the offer, please do not hesitate to contact us.

To accept this offer, please sign and return the enclosed copy of the employment agreement by [Acceptance Deadline]. Upon receipt of your signed agreement, we will initiate the onboarding process and provide you with further instructions on next steps.

We look forward to having you join our team and making valuable contributions to our success. Congratulations on your new position with [Staffing Agency Name].

Sincerely,

[Your Name]
[Title]
[Staffing Agency Name]
[Contact Information]

4. Onboarding Checklist Template:

Pre-Start:
- Send welcome email to new hire with onboarding details
- Provide access to company systems and tools

- Schedule introductory meeting with manager or supervisor
- Prepare workstation and equipment

Day 1:
- Welcome new hire and introduce to team members
- Review company policies, procedures, and culture
- Review job responsibilities and expectations
- Complete new hire paperwork and documentation
- Provide company handbook and resources

First Week:
- Schedule training sessions and orientation activities
- Assign buddy or mentor for guidance and support
- Review job-specific training materials and resources
- Set up meetings with key stakeholders and department heads
- Gather feedback and address any questions or concerns

First Month:
- Conduct performance check-ins and goal-setting discussions

How to start a staffing placement business

- Provide ongoing training and development opportunities
- Review progress and performance against objectives
- Solicit feedback from new hire on onboarding experience
- Address any issues or challenges proactively

Ongoing:
- Provide ongoing support, feedback, and coaching
- Encourage integration and participation in team activities
- Monitor progress and performance and provide recognition for achievements
- Review and update onboarding process based on feedback and lessons learned

By utilizing these recruitment and onboarding templates, staffing agencies can streamline their hiring processes, enhance candidate experience, and ensure successful placements. Customizing the templates to fit specific roles, industries, and organizational needs will help agencies attract top talent, match candidates with

How to start a staffing placement business

suitable job opportunities, and foster long-term success for both clients and candidates.

Appendix IV: Glossary of Terms

1. Staffing Agency:

A staffing agency, also known as a recruitment agency, employment agency, or staffing firm, is a business that matches job seekers with job openings for client companies. Staffing agencies typically source candidates through various channels, screen applicants, and provide temporary, permanent, or contract placements to client organizations across different industries.

2. Temporary Staffing:

Temporary staffing refers to the practice of hiring employees on a short-term basis to fill temporary job openings or address fluctuating staffing needs. Temporary employees, also known as temps or contractors, work for a specified period, often to cover employee absences, seasonal demand, special projects, or peak workload periods.

3. Permanent Placement:

Permanent placement, also known as direct placement or direct hire, involves recruiting and placing candidates in full-time, permanent positions with client companies. Staffing agencies source, screen, and vet candidates on behalf of client organizations, charging a fee or commission upon successful placement.

4. Contract Staffing:

Contract staffing involves placing employees with client companies on a contract basis for a specific duration or project. Contract employees work for the client organization but are employed by the staffing agency, which handles payroll, benefits, and administrative tasks. Contract staffing provides flexibility for clients and opportunities for contractors to gain experience and exposure to different industries.

5. Candidate Sourcing:

Candidate sourcing refers to the process of identifying and attracting potential job candidates for open positions. Staffing agencies use various sourcing methods, including job boards, social media, networking, referrals, and database searches, to source candidates with the required skills, qualifications, and experience.

6. Screening and Assessment:
Screening and assessment involve evaluating candidates' qualifications, skills, experience, and fit for specific job opportunities. Staffing agencies conduct interviews, skills assessments, background checks, reference checks, and drug screenings to ensure candidates meet client requirements and expectations.

7. Talent Pipeline:
A talent pipeline is a pool of qualified candidates who have expressed interest in working with a staffing agency or client organization. Staffing agencies build and maintain talent pipelines through proactive candidate sourcing, networking, and relationship-building activities, enabling quick and efficient placements when job openings arise.

8. Client Acquisition:

Client acquisition refers to the process of identifying, attracting, and acquiring new clients for staffing services. Staffing agencies engage in marketing, sales, networking, and lead generation activities to connect with potential clients, showcase their value proposition, and secure new business opportunities.

9. Client Relationship Management (CRM):
Client relationship management involves building and maintaining positive relationships with client companies to ensure satisfaction, retention, and repeat business. Staffing agencies use CRM software and strategies to track client interactions, manage accounts, and provide personalized service to meet client needs and expectations.

10. Candidate Experience:
Candidate experience refers to the overall perception and satisfaction of job seekers with the recruitment process and interactions with a staffing agency. Providing a positive candidate experience involves clear communication, timely feedback, transparent processes,

and respectful treatment throughout the hiring process, regardless of the outcome.

11. Compliance:

Compliance refers to adherence to laws, regulations, and industry standards governing the recruitment and employment process. Staffing agencies must comply with labor laws, anti-discrimination laws, employment regulations, tax laws, and industry best practices to protect their business interests and maintain ethical standards.

12. Onboarding:

Onboarding is the process of integrating new hires into the organization and providing them with the necessary information, resources, and support to succeed in their roles. Staffing agencies facilitate onboarding for temporary, contract, and permanent placements, ensuring a smooth transition and positive experience for candidates and clients.

13. Payrolling:

Payrolling involves the administration of payroll and related processes for temporary or contract employees placed with client companies. Staffing agencies handle payroll processing, tax withholding, benefits administration, and compliance tasks on behalf of client organizations, simplifying administrative burdens and ensuring accurate and timely payments to workers.

14. Employee Classification:
Employee classification refers to the categorization of workers as either employees or independent contractors for legal and tax purposes. Staffing agencies must properly classify workers based on factors such as control, independence, supervision, and integration into the client's workforce to comply with labor laws and avoid misclassification liabilities.

15. Margin:
Margin, also known as markup, is the difference between the bill rate charged to the client for staffing services and the pay rate paid to the employee or contractor. Staffing agencies use margin to cover overhead costs,

administrative expenses, and profit margins, determining pricing strategies and profitability for each placement.

16. Background Check:
A background check is a process of verifying a candidate's criminal history, employment history, education, and other relevant background information. Staffing agencies conduct background checks to verify candidate credentials, ensure compliance with client requirements, and mitigate risks associated with hiring decisions.

17. Non-Disclosure Agreement (NDA):
A non-disclosure agreement (NDA) is a legal contract between parties to protect confidential information shared during the course of business negotiations or transactions. Staffing agencies use NDAs to safeguard client and candidate information, prevent unauthorized disclosure or use, and maintain confidentiality and trust.

18. Non-Compete Agreement:

A non-compete agreement is a legal contract that prohibits employees or contractors from engaging in competitive activities or working for competitors after leaving the staffing agency or client organization. Non-compete agreements protect the agency's business interests, client relationships, and proprietary information.

19. Arbitration Agreement:
An arbitration agreement is a contract between parties that requires disputes to be resolved through arbitration rather than litigation in court. Staffing agencies use arbitration agreements to streamline dispute resolution, reduce legal costs, and maintain confidentiality in resolving conflicts with clients, candidates, or employees.

By familiarizing yourself with these key terms and concepts, you can navigate the staffing industry more effectively, communicate clearly with clients and candidates, and build a successful staffing agency that

How to start a staffing placement business

delivers value and drives growth in the recruitment industry.

www.ingramcontent.com/pod-product-compliance
Lightning Source LLC
Chambersburg PA
CBHW071923210526
45479CB00002B/533